Crabapples

Sharks

Niki Walker & Bobbie Kalman

Crabtree Publishing Company

www.crabtreebooks.com

Crabapples

created by Bobbie Kalman

For Stephan,
who's a great little "chum"

Editor-in-Chief
Bobbie Kalman

Writing team
Niki Walker
Bobbie Kalman

Managing editor
Lynda Hale

Editors
Petrina Gentile
Greg Nickles

Consultant
Dr. Samuel H. Gruber, Professor,
Rosenstiel School of Marine and
Atmospheric Sciences, University
of Miami, and Director, Bimini
Biological Field Station

Computer design
Lynda Hale
Lucy DeFazio

Photographs
Animals Animals/James Watt: page 15
Wayne and Karen Brown: page 6 (bottom)
Andrew Drake: cover
EarthWater Stock Photography: Chris A. Crumley: pages 4-5;
   Tim Grollimund: page 26; Douglas David Seifert: page 10
Mo Yung Productions: Marjorie Bank: page 24; Bob Cranston:
   title page, page 16; James Watt: pages 20, 28; Norbert Wu:
   pages 13 (top), 17(top), 23, 25, 27
Photo Researchers, Inc.: Douglas Faulkner: page 19 (top left);
   Klaus Hilgert/Okapia: page 18 (right); Noailles Jacana:
   page 17 (bottom); Tom McHugh: page 12;
   Tom McHugh/Steinhart Aquarium: page 13 (bottom);
   Mike Neumann: page 26 (inset)
Jeffrey Rotman: pages 7 (bottom), 11, 18 (left), 21
Tom Stack & Associates: David B. Fleetham: pages 8-9, 19 (bottom);
   Cindy Garoutte: pages 6-7; Randy Morse: page 19 (top right);
   Brian Parker: pages 22, 30

Printer
Worzalla Publishing Company

Color separations and film
Dot 'n Line Image Inc.

Crabtree Publishing Company

PMB 16A
350 Fifth Ave.,
Suite 3308
N.Y., N.Y. 10118

612 Welland Ave.,
St. Catharines,
Ontario, Canada
L2M 5V6

73 Lime Walk
Headington
Oxford OX3 7AD
United Kingdom

Cataloging in Publication Data
Walker, Niki
  Sharks

(Crabapples)
Includes index.

ISBN 0-86505-637-4 (library bound)   ISBN 0-86505-737-0 (pbk.)
This book looks at several aspects of sharks, including their
physiology, reproduction, habitats, diets, and endangerment.

1. Sharks—Juvenile literature. I. Kalman, Bobbie. II. Title.
III. Series: Kalman, Bobbie. Crabapples.

QL638.9.K34 1997   j597.3   LC 97-4089
                                                    CIP

What is in this book?

What are sharks?

Sharks are fish. Most fish are **cold-blooded**. Their body temperature changes with the temperature of the water around them. Fish breathe with organs called **gills**. We breathe with lungs.

There are several differences between sharks and other fish. Most fish have skeletons made of bone. They are called **bony fish**. Sharks are **cartilaginous fish**. Their skeletons are cartilage, which is lighter and more flexible than bone. Our ears are made of cartilage.

There are some things scientists do not know about sharks because these fish are difficult to keep in captivity. Some types starve themselves and die soon after they are captured. Many sharks, especially the larger ones, are hard to study in the wild. It is difficult to watch any animal underwater, and most sharks are fast swimmers that avoid people.

A shark's body

Sharks come in many shapes and sizes. Some are small enough to hold in your hands, and others are longer than a bus! Most sharks, however, are less than five feet long. Sharks are yellow, brown, black, grey, or blue. They may be a solid color or have spots or stripes. Although sharks look different, their bodies have many things in common.

This large **dorsal fin** and the smaller one near the tail keep the shark from rolling over.

A shark pushes itself through the water by sweeping its **caudal fin** from side to side.

Shark skin is rough and scratchy. It is covered with small, toothlike scales called **denticles** that protect the skin from bites and scratches. The size and shape of the denticles differ with each species of shark.

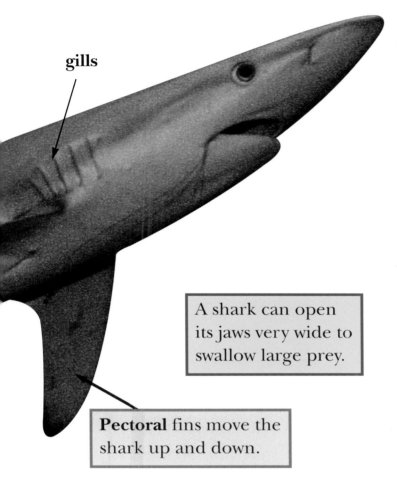

gills

A shark breathes with its gills. The gills take oxygen from the water and release carbon dioxide. Most sharks breathe by swimming with their mouth open, allowing water to flow over their gills. Some sharks lie still and pump water over their gills by opening and closing their mouth.

A shark can open its jaws very wide to swallow large prey.

Sharks cannot chew their food. Some shake their prey until they tear out a chunk of meat and then swallow it whole. Others simply swallow the entire animal or fish at once.

Pectoral fins move the shark up and down.

Some sharks can close their eyelids and others cannot. A few species have a third lid that slides over the eye to protect it when the shark feeds.

A mirror-like layer at the back of the eyes catches and reflects light, helping sharks see at night and in deep water.

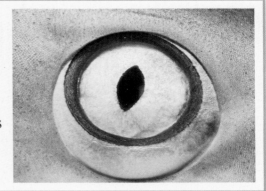

Shark habitats

Sharks can be found in all the oceans of the world except the coldest waters around Antarctica. Most live in the warm, tropical waters around the equator.

Some sharks inhabit the shallow waters near coastlines and coral reefs, and others live in the deep waters of the open ocean. Some types of sharks move between deep and shallow waters.

A few types of sharks can swim in both the salt water of oceans and the fresh water of lakes and rivers. They have been found in tropical lakes and rivers in Africa, South America, Australia, and Southeast Asia. People have also reported seeing bull sharks in the Mississippi River. European fresh waters are too cold for sharks.

What's for dinner?

Many sharks are **top predators**. A predator is an animal that hunts and eats other creatures. Top predators eat many types of animals, but few animals eat them. Large sharks are hunted only by humans, other sharks, and sometimes, orcas.

Sharks hunt mainly other fish, mollusks such as squid and octopus, and crustaceans such as crab and shrimp. They also eat **carrion**, the bodies of animals that are already dead.

Many species are choosy about what they eat. Some, such as hammerheads, even have favorite foods! Hammerheads eat stingrays as often as they can. A stingray is shown on page 18.

When prey becomes scarce, however, most sharks are not picky about food.

Some types of sharks hunt alone, but others hunt in groups, or **schools**. Sharks in schools sometimes compete for prey, but they do not take part in **feeding frenzies** and bite at anything around them, as people once believed. In fact, these sharks are very careful not to bite one another!

11

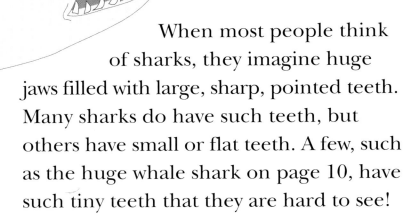

chomp!

When most people think of sharks, they imagine huge jaws filled with large, sharp, pointed teeth. Many sharks do have such teeth, but others have small or flat teeth. A few, such as the huge whale shark on page 10, have such tiny teeth that they are hard to see!

A shark's teeth are suited to the food the shark eats. Some sharks have pointed teeth with sawlike edges that can slice through prey and rip out chunks of meat. Others have pointed teeth that are long and curved to hook fast-moving prey. Sharks that eat shellfish have flat teeth to crack shells. Some sharks have only flat teeth; some have only pointed ones. Others have both kinds.

Sharks have up to seven rows of teeth, but most species use only the outer row. When a tooth falls out, the one behind it moves and replaces it. In some species, whole rows of teeth are replaced at once. Sharks may lose more than 30,000 teeth in their lifetime!

Sense-ational hunters

Scientists once believed that a large part of a shark's brain helped sniff out food. They thought that smell was the shark's most important sense, but now they know this belief is not true. Sharks need all their senses to find food! Hearing is important because sound travels quickly through water and over long distances.

The **lateral line** is an area on a shark's body along which the shark feels vibrations made by other animals swimming in the water. This sense is called **touch-at-a-distance**. Sharks can tell the difference between vibrations made by a healthy creature and those made by one that is weak or injured. Weak and injured animals are easier to catch.

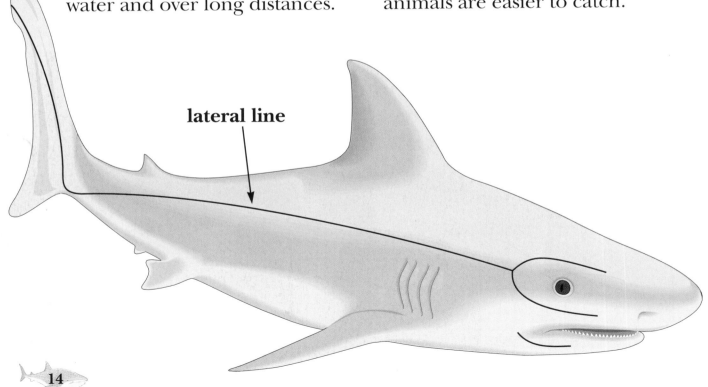

lateral line

A shark uses sight to find nearby prey. Its eyes can spot movement and recognize the difference between light and dark objects, but they cannot see color or shapes very well.

When prey is near its mouth, a shark moves in for the kill by following the animal's **electrical charge**. Every living creature gives off electricity, which the shark feels through small openings on its nose and body. Sharks can feel this electricity better than any other animal!

Baby sharks

A male and female shark **mate** in order to have babies. Before mating, the male follows the female and nips and bites her. The males of some species must be careful because the females are larger and stronger and might kill them.

Shark babies, or **pups**, are born in one of three ways. Some shark mothers carry their pups in a sac inside their body until the babies are ready to be born. Most pups are carried for 10 to 12 months, but some are carried for almost two years!

Most pups hatch from eggs inside their mother's body. In one species, the sand tiger shark, there may be 20 or more eggs, but only two babies leave the mother alive. The first few babies to hatch feed on the unhatched eggs and then fight and eat one another until only two are left.

In other species, shark pups hatch from eggs laid by their mother. A leathery **egg case**, known as a "mermaid's pouch," protects the eggs from predators. Some cases have long strands at the ends, and they become tangled around rocks or plants. The strands hold the egg case in one spot.

No matter how they are born, most pups look like small versions of adult sharks. They have teeth and can hunt and care for themselves. Mothers leave right after laying eggs or giving birth.

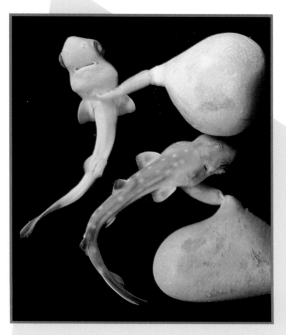

These pups grow inside their mother's body.

This young shark just hatched from a nearby egg case.

17

Sharks and relatives

Sharks are related to skates and rays. Sharks and their relatives are called **elasmobranchs**. These animals all have cartilage skeletons.

Scientists believe ancient sharks began living on earth about 400 million years ago. Ancestors of today's sharks probably appeared 100 million years ago.

Sharks have changed a lot over millions of years, but they have kept their useful, streamlined body shape. Fossil teeth from ancestors look like the teeth of today's sharks, but some are much larger.

Scientists are uncertain how many species of sharks there are in the world, but they believe there are at least 370.

fossil jaw and teeth

stingray

The pictures below show just a few of the many different species of sharks.

horn shark

leopard shark

wobbegong

Great whites

The great white shark is also known as the white shark, white pointer, and white death. These sharks have been found in all the oceans, in both deep and shallow water. They are most common, however, in cool waters where there are lots of seals and sea lions to hunt.

Great whites also eat salmon, tuna, dolphins, porpoises, other sharks, and the bodies of dead whales. They are known to **spy hop**, or poke their head above the surface of the water to look for prey.

A great white surprises its prey by attacking it from behind and below. It usually takes a single bite and then moves away, waiting for the animal to bleed to death. Some scientists believe that, after a large meal, a great white can wait up to one month before eating again!

Hammerheads

Scientists are not certain why the heads of hammerheads are shaped the way they are. Some think the wide head helps these sharks smell and feel electrical charges better Others think it helps the sharks turn quickly when chasing prey.

Hammerheads hunt small fish, other sharks, crustaceans, and stingrays. They usually hunt at night.

There are eight species of hammerheads. The smallest is the bonnethead. The largest is the great hammerhead.

Hammerheads live in warm, shallow ocean waters around the world. One species, the scalloped hammerhead, **migrates**, or travels long distances, twice each year. The sharks swim south in winter and north in summer.

Tiger sharks

Tiger sharks are named for the stripes they have along their sides while they are young. They are often called the "trash cans of the sea" or "swimming garbage cans" because they will eat almost anything. Tiger sharks have been found with tin cans, old boots, and license plates in their stomach!

Tiger sharks spend much of their time in the deep waters near the edges of coral reefs. They swim into shallow waters to hunt lobster, squid, fish, sea turtles, birds, and smaller sharks. Tiger sharks have also been known to eat people! They are among the few species of human-eating sharks.

Bull sharks

The bull shark is one of the few species that can move between the salt water of oceans and the fresh water of rivers and lakes. It is aggressive and has been blamed for most of the attacks on swimmers in fresh water. Bull sharks are also believed to be the most dangerous sharks in tropical waters. Some experts suspect they cause many of the attacks that people blame on great whites.

Bull sharks feed on a wide variety of prey, including small fish, other sharks, dolphins, and sea turtles. Hippos, antelopes, cattle, and dogs have also been found in the stomach of these sharks.

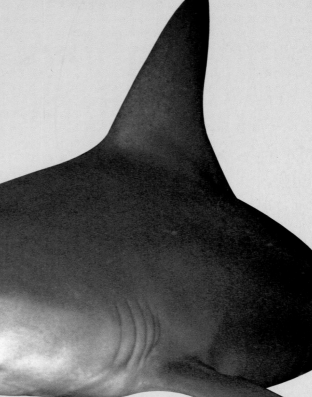

Whale sharks

Whale sharks are the largest fish in the world. They are nicknamed "gentle giants" because they have never been known to attack people.

Whale sharks are found in warm oceans and seas. They have been seen swimming alone and in schools of more than a hundred sharks.

The whale shark is one of the three species of sharks known to be **filter feeders**. Their gills are covered with thousands of tiny hooks called **gill rakers**. To eat, filter feeders simply swim with their mouth open. As water passes over their gill rakers, plankton, shrimp, and small fish get caught on these filters.

Cookie-cutter sharks

The cookie-cutter shark spends the day in deep waters and comes to the surface to hunt at night. Some scientists think its body can glow bright green, possibly to attract prey.

Even though it is small, the cookie-cutter shark feeds on larger prey such as whales, seals, tuna, and other sharks. It uses its large lips like a suction cup and sticks itself to its prey. The little shark then sucks in a mouthful of flesh and twists its body. As it turns, its razor-sharp teeth cut out the flesh in the same way a cookie cutter cuts out a cookie from dough.

Nurse sharks

Nurse sharks are **bottom dwellers**. They spend their life in shallow water, near the sandy ocean bottom. During the day, nurse sharks lie in dark spots, often piling on top of one another. At night, they come out to hunt.

Nurse sharks eat crabs, shrimp, lobsters, sea urchins, and fish. They have two feelers, or **barbels**, which hang from either side of their mouth. They may use their barbels to search for prey hidden in the sand. If the prey is wedged between two rocks, a nurse shark places its large lips over the hole and sucks out the animal like a vacuum cleaner.

Swell sharks

Swell sharks are named for their ability to swell, or puff up. When this small shark is in danger, it swims into a crevice and swallows water. Its stomach swells so much that the shark cannot be pulled from its hiding place!

When swell sharks are caught and pulled onto a boat, they sometimes swallow air and puff up to protect themselves. They let out the air from their stomach in small burps and sound as if they are barking!

Swell sharks are found in the Pacific Ocean, along the coasts of California, Mexico, Chile, Japan, and Australia.

Shark attack!

Many people fear shark attacks, but a person is more likely to be killed by a dog or a bee sting than harmed by a shark. Only 50 of the 370 species of sharks are large or strong enough to harm people. Great whites, tigers, bulls, hammerheads, and oceanic whitetip sharks are blamed for most of the attacks.

Scientists once believed in **rogue sharks**. Rogue sharks were thought to be loners that had a taste for people. Many people still think sharks are mindless killers that attack humans to eat them, but scientists are learning that this old belief is not true!

Scientists now think most attacks are caused by people poking sharks, moving into their territory, making them feel threatened, or flashing cameras in their face. Sometimes sharks attack when there is blood in the water, either from a wounded person or fish.

Great whites seem to mistake people paddling on surfboards for prey. From below, a surfboard with a person's arms and legs dangling around it may look like a seal or sea lion. When the shark tastes the person's flesh, it usually spits it out and stops the attack.

Sharks in trouble

Sharks help keep oceans healthy by eating sick animals. They are also useful to people. Some are eaten, and the skin of others is used as leather. Scientists are studying sharks because these animals do not seem to get cancer. Something in a shark's body may cure cancer in people.

Sharks may help us, but we are their worst enemies. At least 100 million sharks are caught each year for food and fun. One of the greatest wastes of sharks is **finning**. People catch sharks, cut off their fins, and throw their bodies into the water to bleed to death. People pay a lot of money for the fins, which are used to make sharkfin soup.

We kill sharks faster than they are being born, and many species are in danger of becoming **extinct**. Scientists fear that in 100 years, species that have been on earth for millions of years will be gone forever.

Words to know

aggressive Describing an animal that is often hostile towards others

ancestor An early animal from which later species developed

ancient Describing something that existed long ago

carbon dioxide A gas that animals breathe out

cartilage A tough but flexible tissue that is also called gristle

fossil The remains, such as teeth or bones, of an animal that lived long ago

mate The act of a male and female animal joining together to produce young

oxygen A gas that animals need to breathe

predator An animal that hunts and eats other animals

prey An animal that is hunted and eaten by another animal

school A group of fish

species A group of animals whose members share features of behavior and appearance

streamlined Describing something that is shaped to move through air or water with little resistance

vibration A quick movement or shaking of the ground, air, water, or other objects

Index

What is in the picture?

Here is more information about the photographs in this book.

page:		page:	
cover	Blue sharks live in all the oceans.	18 (right)	Stingrays have a poisonous tip on the end of their tail.
title page	Blue sharks are also called blue whalers.	19 (top left)	Leopard sharks are up to 5 feet (1.5 m) long.
4-5	A Caribbean reef shark	19 (top right)	Horn sharks are named for the sharp spine near their dorsal fin.
6-7	Blue sharks are up to 12 feet (4 m) long.	19 (bottom)	Wobbegongs lie on reefs and sandy bottoms to wait for prey.
6	This skin belongs to a basking shark, the second-largest shark.	20	Great whites can be longer than 19 feet (6 m) and weigh more than 4,800 pounds (2 500 kg)!
7	The eye of a lemon shark		
8-9	A whitetip reef shark	21	The shape of their head may protect hammerheads' eyes from the stinging tails of stingrays.
10	Whale sharks are found in warm waters around the world.		
11	Reef sharks grab at bait, or **chum**, that was dropped in the water.	22	Tiger sharks are the largest predators in coral reefs.
12	The carpet shark has tiny teeth!	23	Bull sharks are one of the three species most often blamed for attacks on people.
13 (top)	Although it looks fierce, the sand tiger shark is not a threat to swimmers.		
13 (bottom)	The jawbone and teeth of a great white shark	24	Whale sharks can be 40 feet (12 m) long!
15	Sensitive openings on the snout of a shark help it sense prey.	25	Cookie-cutter sharks are less than 20 inches (51 cm) long.
16	A swell shark pup is hatched from an egg case.	26	Nurse sharks are found in the Atlantic Ocean and can be over 13 feet (4 m) long.
17 (top)	Some pups are attached to sacs that give them food as they grow.	26 (inset)	A nurse shark's barbels
17 (bottom)	Behind the pup, there is an egg still in its case.	27	Swell sharks are 3 ft. (1 m) long.
18 (left)	Scientists believe the ancestors of great white sharks had larger jaws than those of great whites.	28	Scientists think there are fewer than 100 great whites in U.S. waters.
		30	These sharks were caught during a fishing tournament.

4 5 6 7 8 9 0 Printed in USA 6 5 4 3 2 1